_____

_____

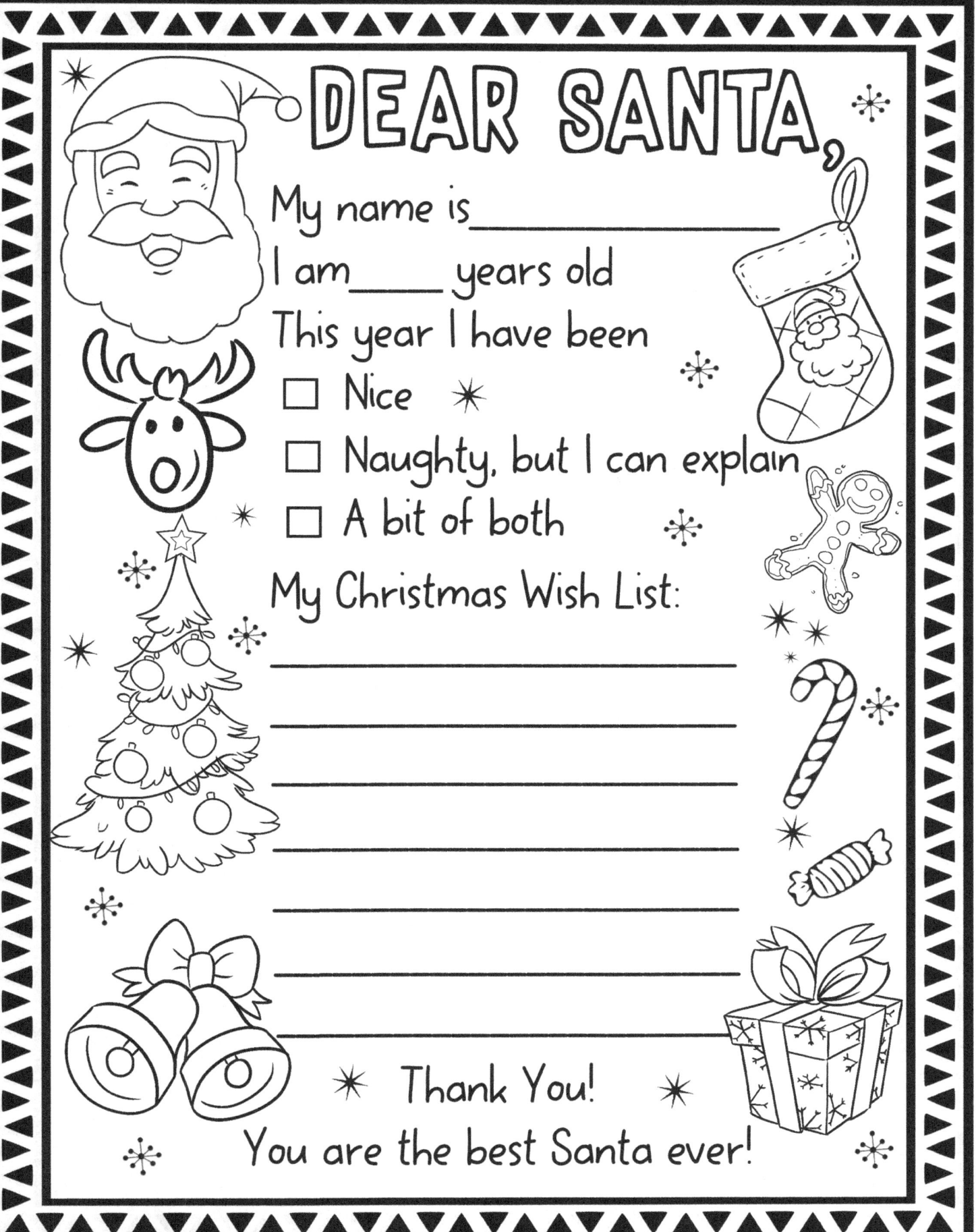

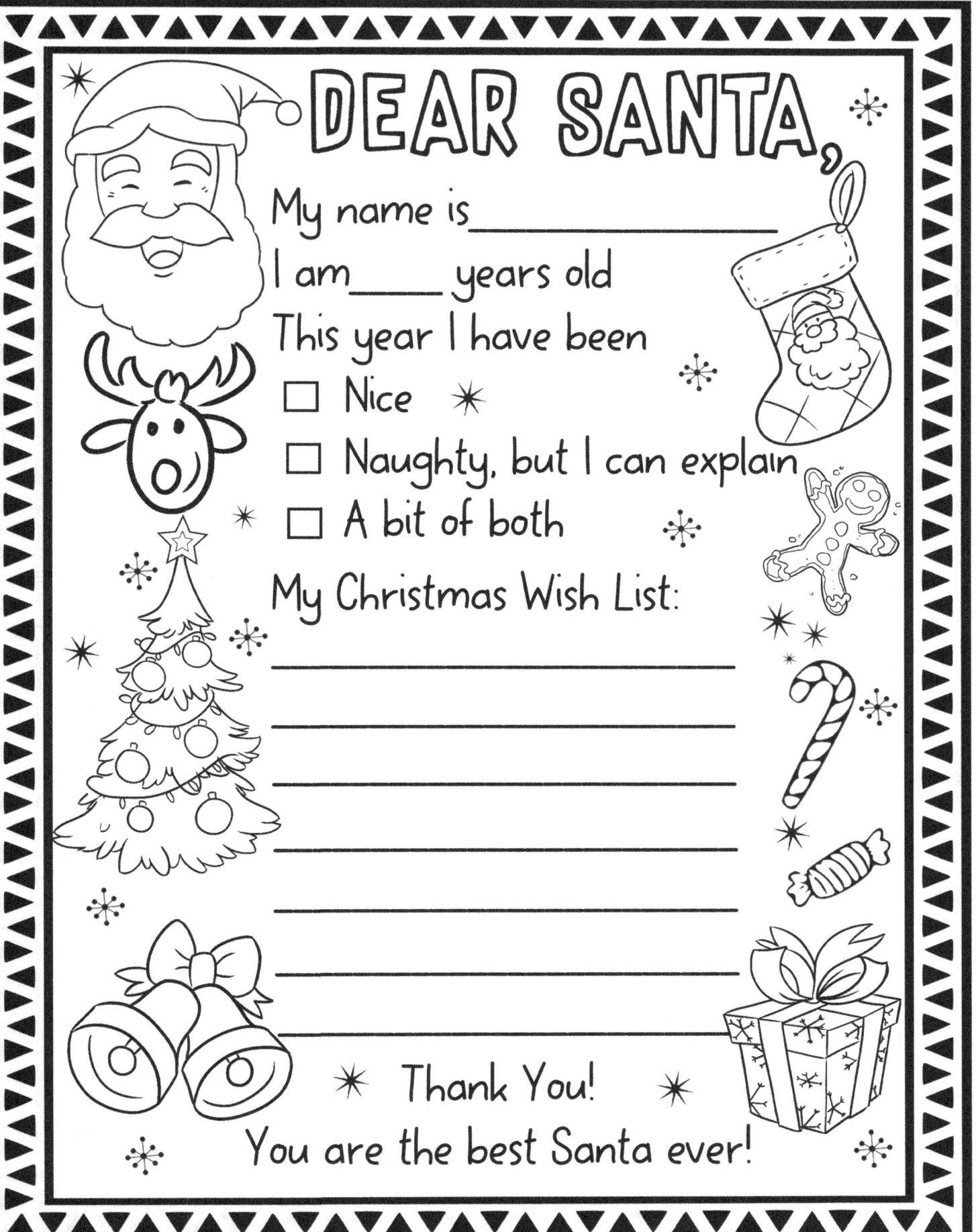

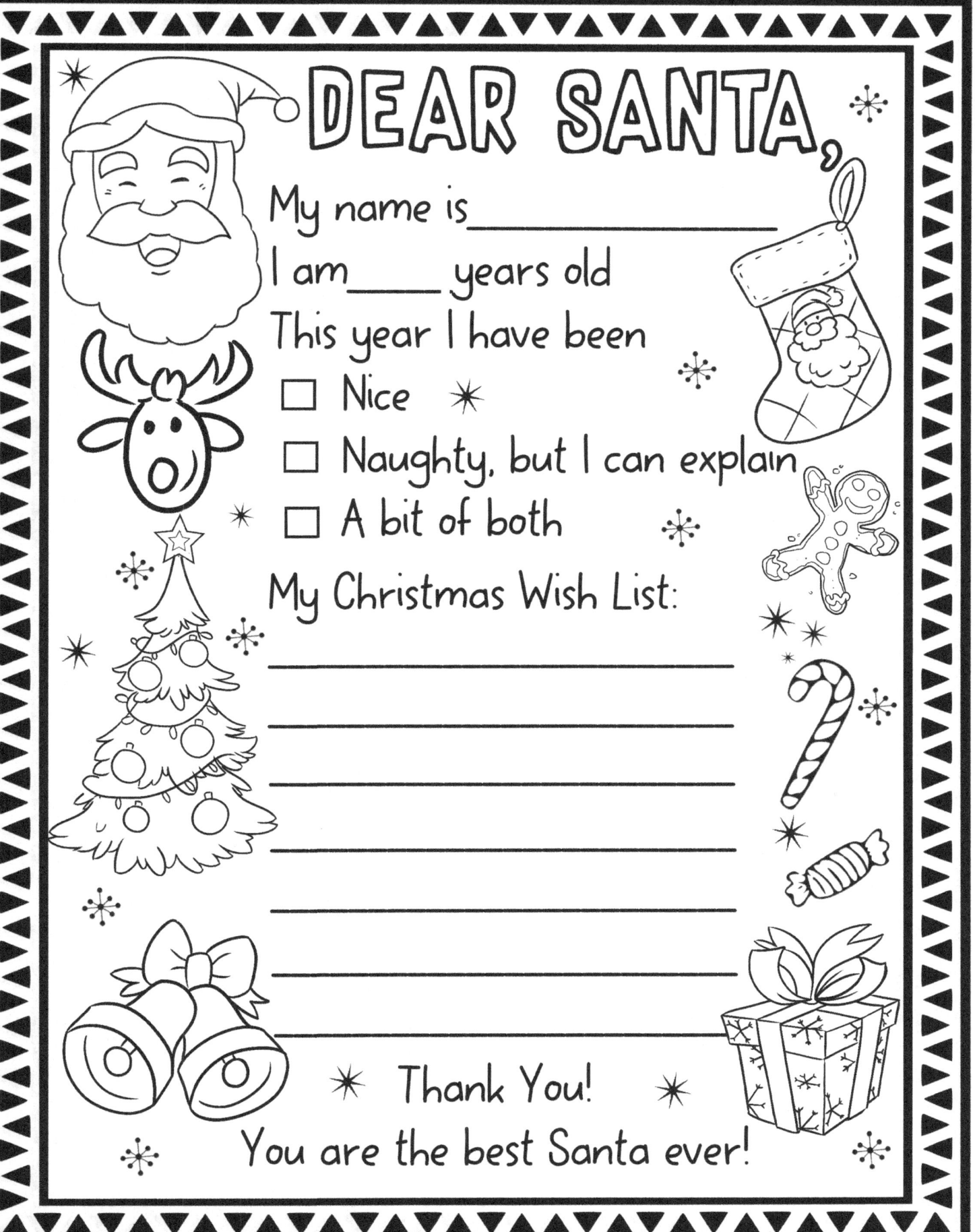

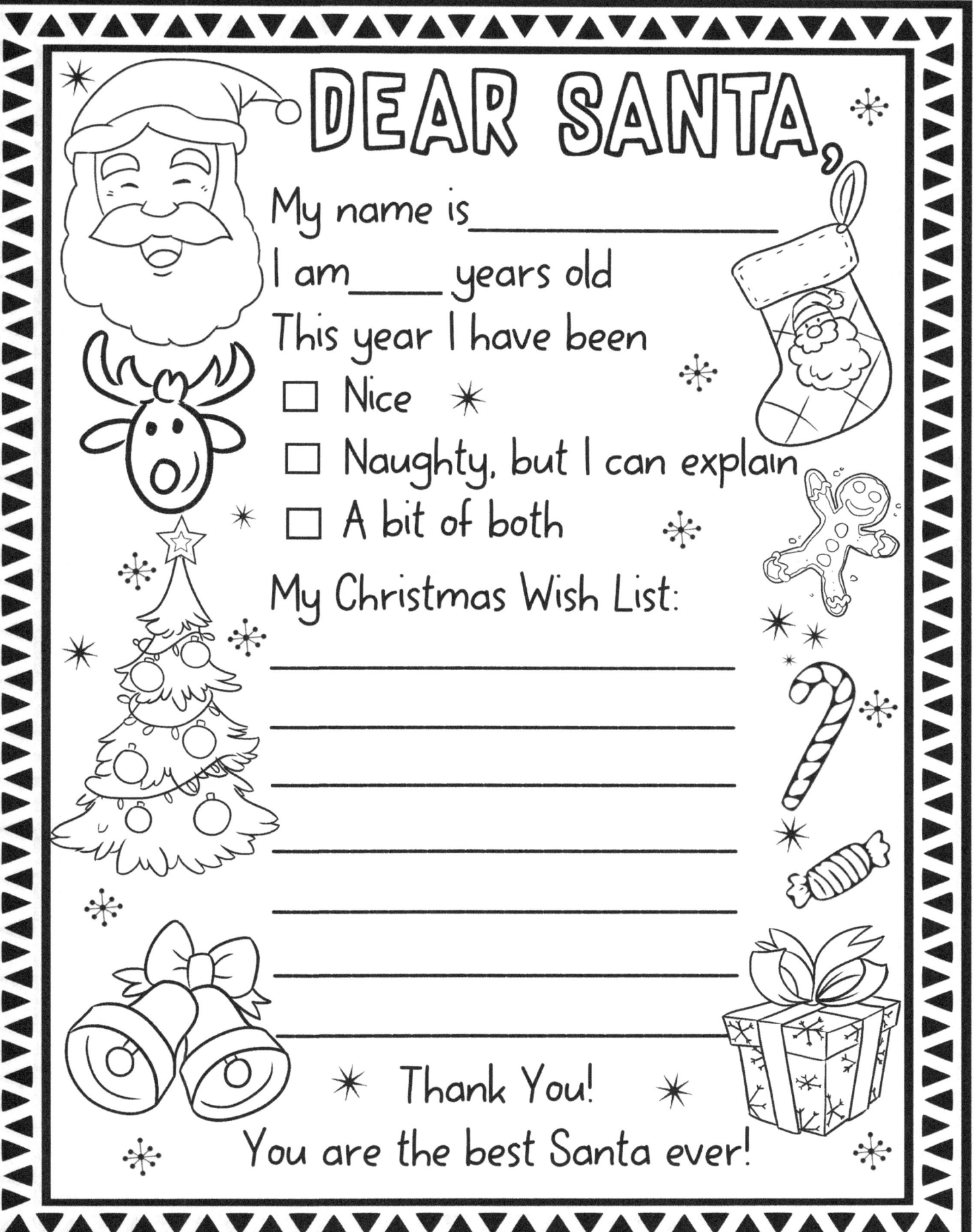

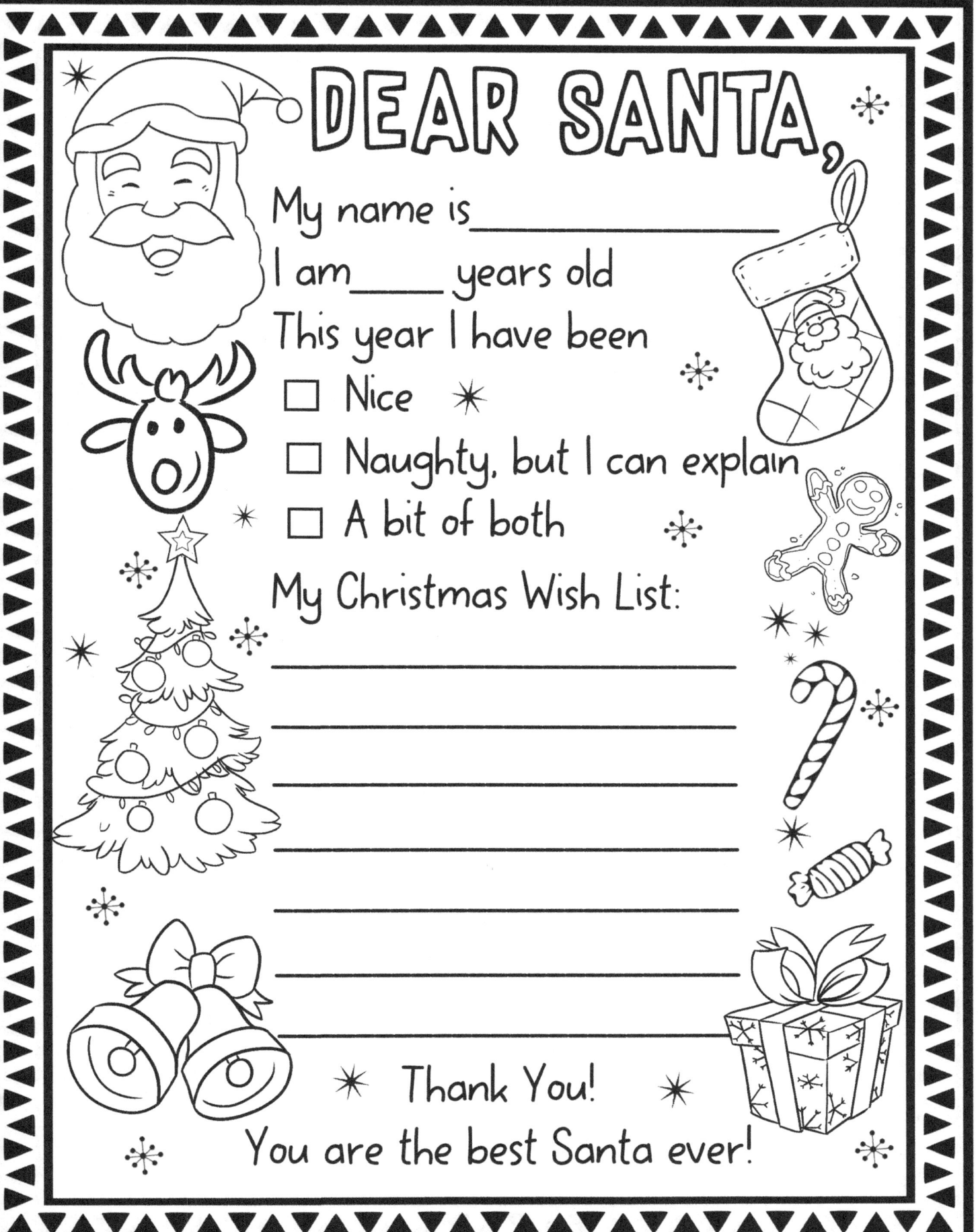

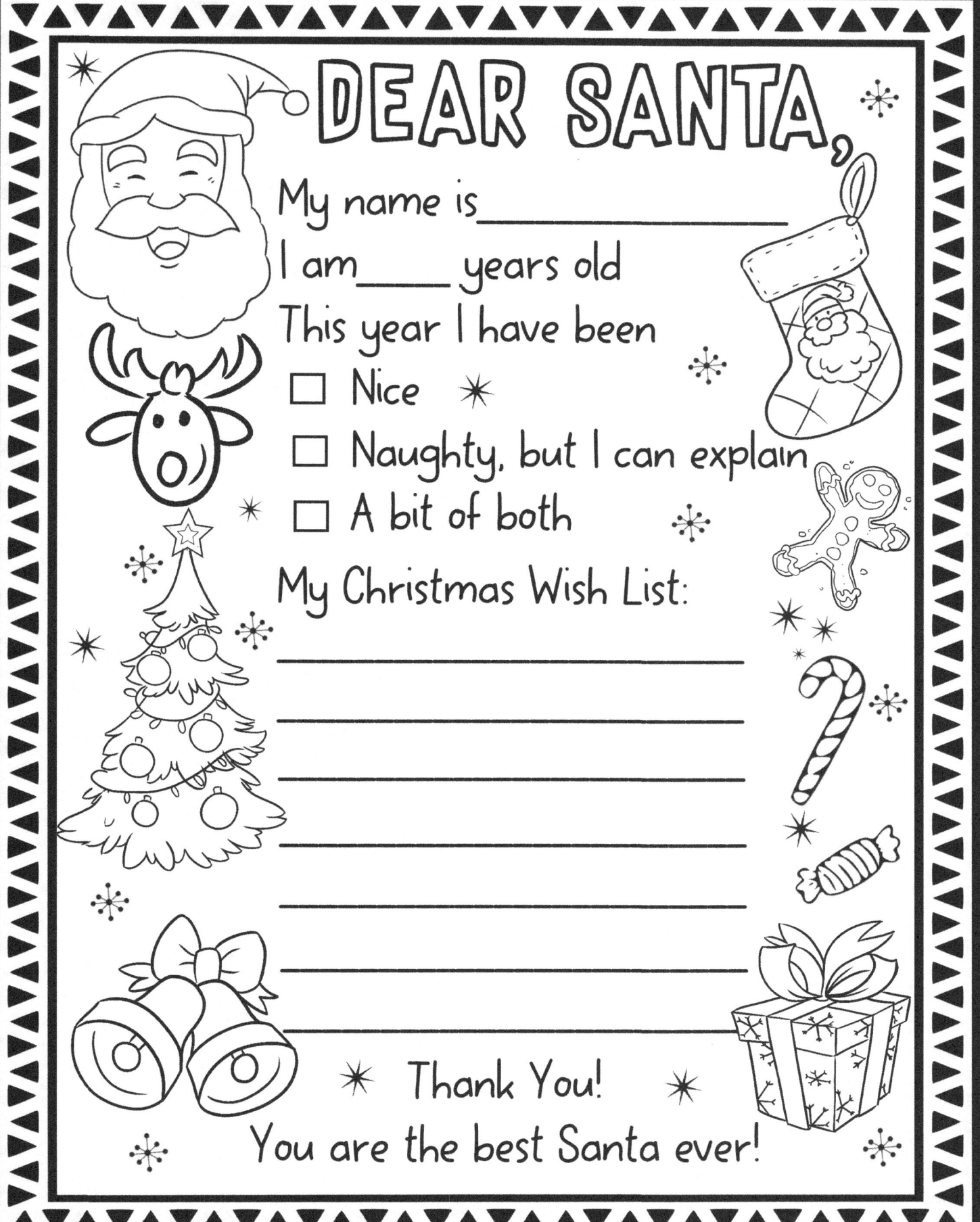

DEAR SANTA,

My name is _____

I am ____ years old

This year I have been

☐ Nice

☐ Naughty, but I can explain

☐ A bit of both

My Christmas Wish List:

_____

_____

_____

_____

_____

_____

Thank You!
You are the best Santa ever!

DEAR SANTA,

My name is _____

I am ____ years old

This year I have been

☐ Nice

☐ Naughty, but I can explain

☐ A bit of both

My Christmas Wish List:

_____

_____

_____

_____

_____

_____

Thank You!
You are the best Santa ever!

DEAR SANTA,

My name is _____

I am ____ years old

This year I have been

☐ Nice

☐ Naughty, but I can explain

☐ A bit of both

My Christmas Wish List:

_____

_____

_____

_____

_____

_____

Thank You!
You are the best Santa ever!

DEAR SANTA,

My name is _____

I am ____ years old

This year I have been

☐ Nice

☐ Naughty, but I can explain

☐ A bit of both

My Christmas Wish List:

_____
_____
_____
_____
_____
_____

Thank You!
You are the best Santa ever!

DEAR SANTA,

My name is _____

I am ____ years old

This year I have been

☐ Nice

☐ Naughty, but I can explain

☐ A bit of both

My Christmas Wish List:

_____

_____

_____

_____

_____

Thank You!
You are the best Santa ever!

DEAR SANTA,

My name is _____

I am ____ years old

This year I have been
- ☐ Nice
- ☐ Naughty, but I can explain
- ☐ A bit of both

My Christmas Wish List:

_____
_____
_____
_____
_____
_____

Thank You!
You are the best Santa ever!

DEAR SANTA,

My name is _____

I am _____ years old

This year I have been
- ☐ Nice
- ☐ Naughty, but I can explain
- ☐ A bit of both

My Christmas Wish List:

_____

_____

_____

_____

_____

Thank You!
You are the best Santa ever!

DEAR SANTA,

My name is _____

I am ____ years old

This year I have been

☐ Nice

☐ Naughty, but I can explain

☐ A bit of both

My Christmas Wish List:

_____
_____
_____
_____
_____
_____

Thank You!
You are the best Santa ever!

DEAR SANTA,

My name is _____

I am ____ years old

This year I have been

☐ Nice

☐ Naughty, but I can explain

☐ A bit of both

My Christmas Wish List:

_____

_____

_____

_____

_____

_____

Thank You!
You are the best Santa ever!

DEAR SANTA,

My name is _____

I am ____ years old

This year I have been

☐ Nice

☐ Naughty, but I can explain

☐ A bit of both

My Christmas Wish List:

_____
_____
_____
_____
_____
_____

Thank You!
You are the best Santa ever!

DEAR SANTA,

My name is _____

I am _____ years old

This year I have been
- ☐ Nice
- ☐ Naughty, but I can explain
- ☐ A bit of both

My Christmas Wish List:

_____

_____

_____

_____

_____

Thank You!
You are the best Santa ever!

DEAR SANTA,

My name is _____

I am ____ years old

This year I have been
- ☐ Nice
- ☐ Naughty, but I can explain
- ☐ A bit of both

My Christmas Wish List:

_____
_____
_____
_____
_____
_____

Thank You!
You are the best Santa ever!

DEAR SANTA,

My name is _____

I am ____ years old

This year I have been
- ☐ Nice
- ☐ Naughty, but I can explain
- ☐ A bit of both

My Christmas Wish List:

_____
_____
_____
_____
_____

Thank You!
You are the best Santa ever!

DEAR SANTA,

My name is _____

I am ____ years old

This year I have been

☐ Nice

☐ Naughty, but I can explain

☐ A bit of both

My Christmas Wish List:

_____
_____
_____
_____
_____

Thank You!
You are the best Santa ever!

DEAR SANTA,

My name is _____

I am ____ years old

This year I have been

☐ Nice

☐ Naughty, but I can explain

☐ A bit of both

My Christmas Wish List:

_____

_____

_____

_____

_____

_____

Thank You!
You are the best Santa ever!

DEAR SANTA,

My name is _____

I am _____ years old

This year I have been

☐ Nice

☐ Naughty, but I can explain

☐ A bit of both

My Christmas Wish List:

_____

_____

_____

_____

_____

Thank You!
You are the best Santa ever!

DEAR SANTA,

My name is _____

I am ____ years old

This year I have been
- ☐ Nice
- ☐ Naughty, but I can explain
- ☐ A bit of both

My Christmas Wish List:

_____

_____

_____

_____

_____

_____

Thank You!
You are the best Santa ever!

DEAR SANTA,

My name is _____

I am ____ years old

This year I have been
- ☐ Nice
- ☐ Naughty, but I can explain
- ☐ A bit of both

My Christmas Wish List:

_____
_____
_____
_____
_____
_____

Thank You!
You are the best Santa ever!

DEAR SANTA,

My name is _____

I am _____ years old

This year I have been

☐ Nice

☐ Naughty, but I can explain

☐ A bit of both

My Christmas Wish List:

_____

_____

_____

_____

_____

_____

Thank You!
You are the best Santa ever!

DEAR SANTA,

My name is _____

I am _____ years old

This year I have been
- ☐ Nice
- ☐ Naughty, but I can explain
- ☐ A bit of both

My Christmas Wish List:

_____
_____
_____
_____
_____
_____

Thank You!
You are the best Santa ever!

DEAR SANTA,

My name is _____

I am ____ years old

This year I have been

☐ Nice

☐ Naughty, but I can explain

☐ A bit of both

My Christmas Wish List:

_____

_____

_____

_____

_____

_____

Thank You!
You are the best Santa ever!

DEAR SANTA,

My name is _____

I am ____ years old

This year I have been
- ☐ Nice
- ☐ Naughty, but I can explain
- ☐ A bit of both

My Christmas Wish List:

_____
_____
_____
_____
_____
_____

Thank You!
You are the best Santa ever!

DEAR SANTA,

My name is _____

I am ____ years old

This year I have been

☐ Nice

☐ Naughty, but I can explain

☐ A bit of both

My Christmas Wish List:

_____

_____

_____

_____

_____

_____

Thank You!
You are the best Santa ever!

DEAR SANTA,

My name is _____

I am ____ years old

This year I have been

☐ Nice

☐ Naughty, but I can explain

☐ A bit of both

My Christmas Wish List:

_____
_____
_____
_____
_____
_____

Thank You!
You are the best Santa ever!

DEAR SANTA,

My name is _____

I am ____ years old

This year I have been

☐ Nice

☐ Naughty, but I can explain

☐ A bit of both

My Christmas Wish List:

_____

_____

_____

_____

_____

_____

Thank You!
You are the best Santa ever!

DEAR SANTA,

My name is _____

I am ____ years old

This year I have been

☐ Nice

☐ Naughty, but I can explain

☐ A bit of both

My Christmas Wish List:

_____
_____
_____
_____
_____
_____

Thank You!
You are the best Santa ever!

DEAR SANTA,

My name is _____

I am ____ years old

This year I have been

☐ Nice

☐ Naughty, but I can explain

☐ A bit of both

My Christmas Wish List:

_____
_____
_____
_____
_____
_____

Thank You!
You are the best Santa ever!

DEAR SANTA,

My name is _____

I am ____ years old

This year I have been
- ☐ Nice
- ☐ Naughty, but I can explain
- ☐ A bit of both

My Christmas Wish List:

_____
_____
_____
_____
_____
_____

Thank You!
You are the best Santa ever!

DEAR SANTA,

My name is _____

I am ____ years old

This year I have been
- ☐ Nice
- ☐ Naughty, but I can explain
- ☐ A bit of both

My Christmas Wish List:

_____

_____

_____

_____

_____

Thank You!
You are the best Santa ever!

DEAR SANTA,

My name is _____

I am ____ years old

This year I have been
- ☐ Nice
- ☐ Naughty, but I can explain
- ☐ A bit of both

My Christmas Wish List:

_____
_____
_____
_____
_____
_____

Thank You!
You are the best Santa ever!

DEAR SANTA,

My name is _____

I am _____ years old

This year I have been

☐ Nice

☐ Naughty, but I can explain

☐ A bit of both

My Christmas Wish List:

_____

_____

_____

_____

_____

_____

Thank You!
You are the best Santa ever!

DEAR SANTA,

My name is _____

I am ____ years old

This year I have been
- ☐ Nice
- ☐ Naughty, but I can explain
- ☐ A bit of both

My Christmas Wish List:

_____
_____
_____
_____
_____
_____

Thank You!
You are the best Santa ever!

DEAR SANTA,

My name is _____

I am ____ years old

This year I have been

☐ Nice

☐ Naughty, but I can explain

☐ A bit of both

My Christmas Wish List:

_____
_____
_____
_____
_____

Thank You!
You are the best Santa ever!

DEAR SANTA,

My name is _____

I am ____ years old

This year I have been
- ☐ Nice
- ☐ Naughty, but I can explain
- ☐ A bit of both

My Christmas Wish List:

_____
_____
_____
_____
_____
_____

Thank You!
You are the best Santa ever!

DEAR SANTA,

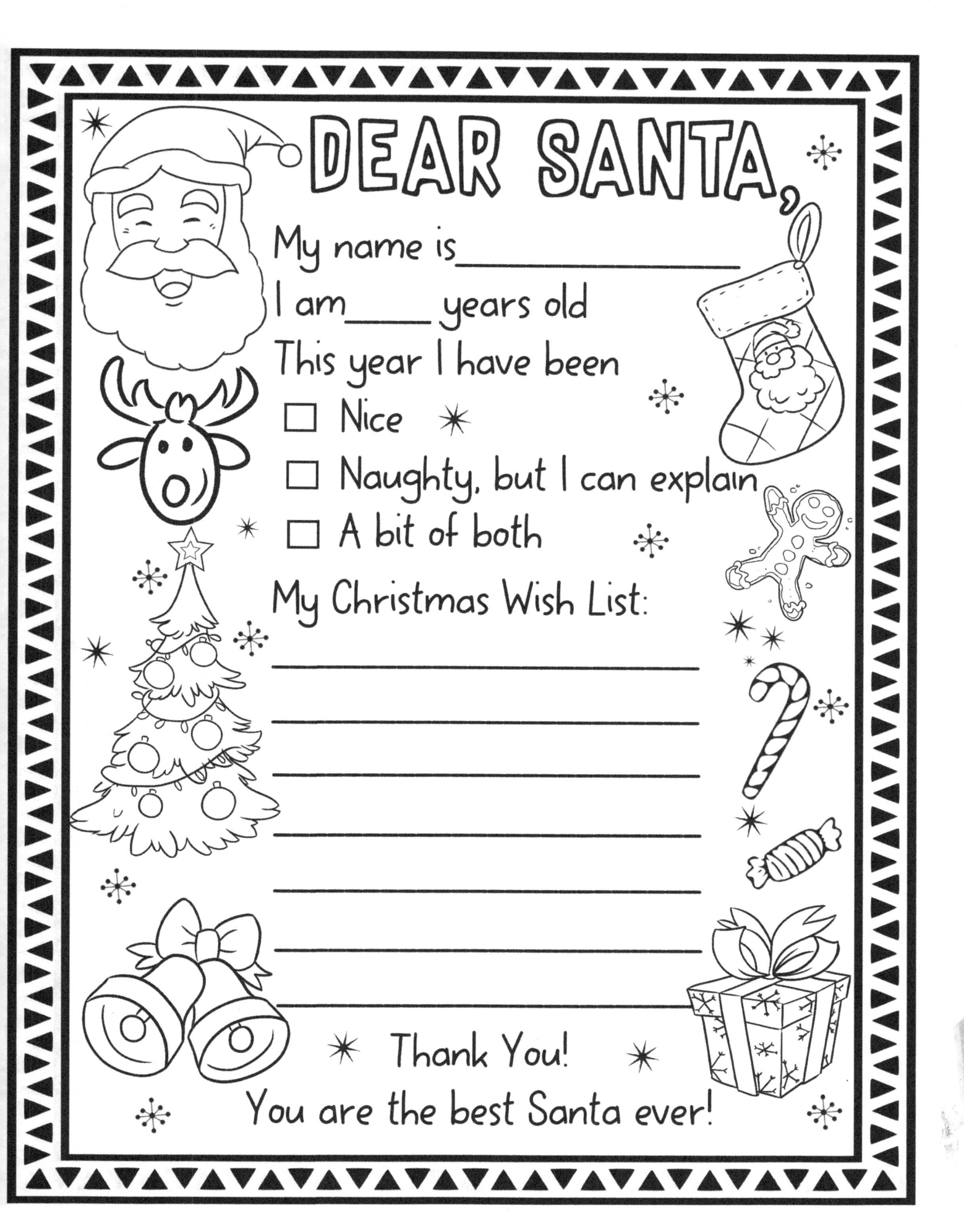

My name is _____

I am ____ years old

This year I have been

☐ Nice

☐ Naughty, but I can explain

☐ A bit of both

My Christmas Wish List:

_____
_____
_____
_____
_____
_____

Thank You!
You are the best Santa ever!

DEAR SANTA,

My name is _____

I am ____ years old

This year I have been
- ☐ Nice
- ☐ Naughty, but I can explain
- ☐ A bit of both

My Christmas Wish List:

_____
_____
_____
_____
_____
_____
_____

Thank You!
You are the best Santa ever!

Made in the USA
Las Vegas, NV
09 December 2023